Microsoft Surface Application Sketch Book

For Windows 8.x Apps on the Surface Pro and
Windows RT Apps on SurfaceTablets

Dean Kaplan

Apress®

Microsoft Surface Application Sketch Book

ISBN-13 (pbk): 978-1-4302-6649-5

President and Publisher: Paul Manning

Lead Editor: Jeffrey Pepper
Editorial Board: Steve Anglin, Mark Beckner, Ewan Buckingham, Gary Cornell, Louise Corrigan, Jonathan Gennick, Jonathan Hassell, Robert Hutchinson, Michelle Lowman, James Markham, Matthew Moodie, Jeff Olson, Jeffrey Pepper, Douglas Pundick, Ben Renow-Clarke, Dominic Shakeshaft, Gwenan Spearing, Matt Wade
Coordinating Editor: Kevin Shea
Compositor: SPi Global
Indexer: SPi Global
Cover Designer: Anna Ishchenko

Distributed to the book trade worldwide by Springer Science+Business Media New York, 233 Spring Street, 6th Floor, New York, NY 10013. Phone 1-800-SPRINGER, fax (201) 348-4505, e-mail **orders-ny@springer-sbm.com**, or visit **www.springeronline.com**. Apress Media, LLC is a California LLC and the sole member (owner) is Springer Science + Business Media Finance Inc (SSBM Finance Inc). SSBM Finance Inc is a Delaware corporation.

For information on translations, please e-mail **rights@apress.com**, or visit **www.apress.com**.

Apress and friends of ED books may be purchased in bulk for academic, corporate, or promotional use. eBook versions and licenses are also available for most titles. For more information, reference our Special Bulk Sales–eBook Licensing web page at **www.apress.com/bulk-sales**.

Any source code or other supplementary materials referenced by the author in this text is available to readers at www.apress.com. For detailed information about how to locate your book's source code, go to **www.apress.com/source-code/**.

Introduction

The *Microsoft Surface Application Sketch Book* is the brainchild of Dean Kaplan who understood the need of smartphone application designers for a place to sketch and keep sketches of their design ideas. He has taken this idea and transferred it to the Microsoft Surface platforms. With the knowledge that people often write their ideas on a whiteboard, only to lose them or other important details later, we created a sketchbook appropriate for the Microsoft Surface.

The idea, of course, is really simple. Give the user 150 pages of grid space to draw or layout their plans, sketches or whatever, for their Surface applications. Users have found a number of unexpected uses for the book.

The book features:

- A grid background on each page.
- A lay flat binding so that you can have a hand on your Surface and one on a pencil.
- 150 pages to write, draw, compose or doodle on.
- An organized place for your user interface designs.

To use the lay flat binding, simply open the book to the page you wish and in the gutter crease both pages with your hand.

We hope that you will find the book useful for whatever purpose you choose.

About the Author

Dean Kaplan is founder and owner of Kapsoft, a technology consulting firm specializing in software applications for engineering applications. Kapsoft provides a full spectrum of product design and development services including manufacturing automation, cellular and location services, material handling, automatic identification, network analysis and protocols, telecommunications, telecom billing, healthcare, and bond trading. Dean recently designed and executed a new synthetic instrument product serving as a replacement for five or more legacy RF test instruments.

Dean anticipated a need for simple effective smartphone design tools and created Application Sketch Books for the iPhone and the iPad to fill that void. Kapsoft is currently deeply involved in new exciting accessory development for the various smartphone platforms including the creation of stencils. More information about other related Kapsoft smartphone products may be obtained at mobilestencil.com.

Dean Kaplan was born in Philadelphia and to this day still resides in nearby Haverford, Pennsylvania. Dean has a Bachelor of Science in Electrical Engineering Technology obtained from Temple University in 1982. Dean writes a contemporary technology blog at DeanOnSoftware.com. For info about Kapsoft, please see Kapsoft.com. You can also follow Dean on Twitter at @Kapsoft.

 Kapsoft

Application Name:

Screen Name:

Notes:

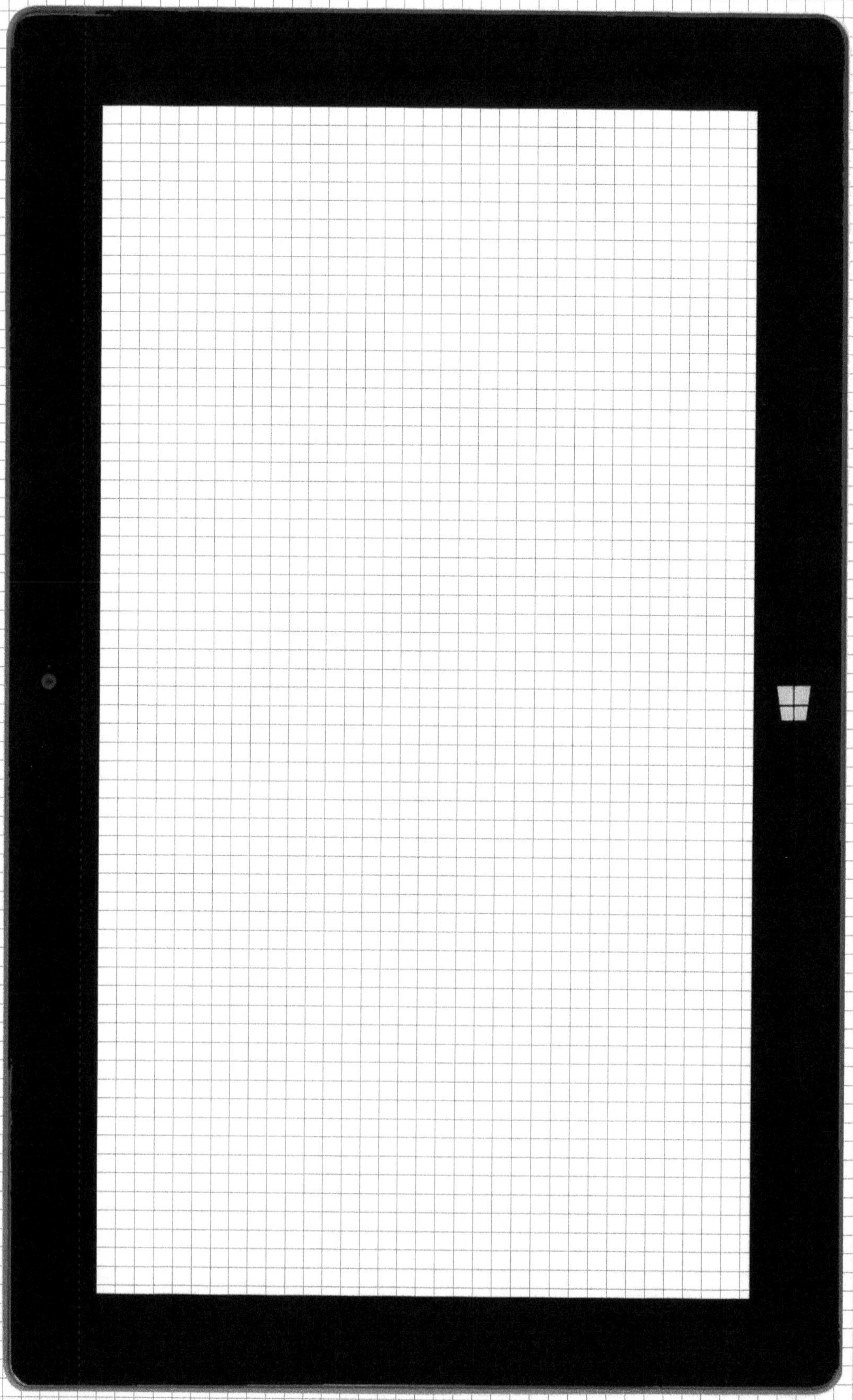

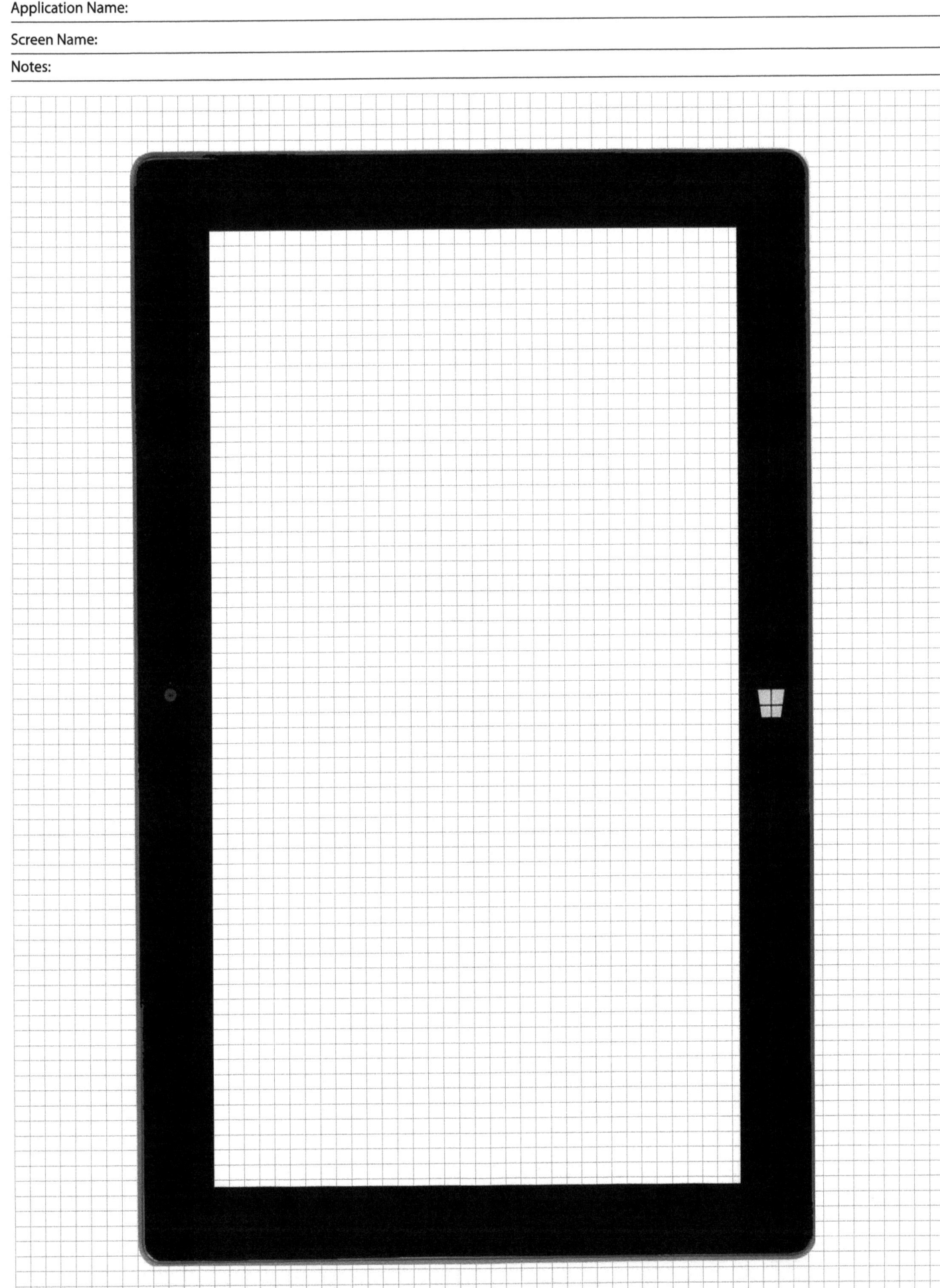

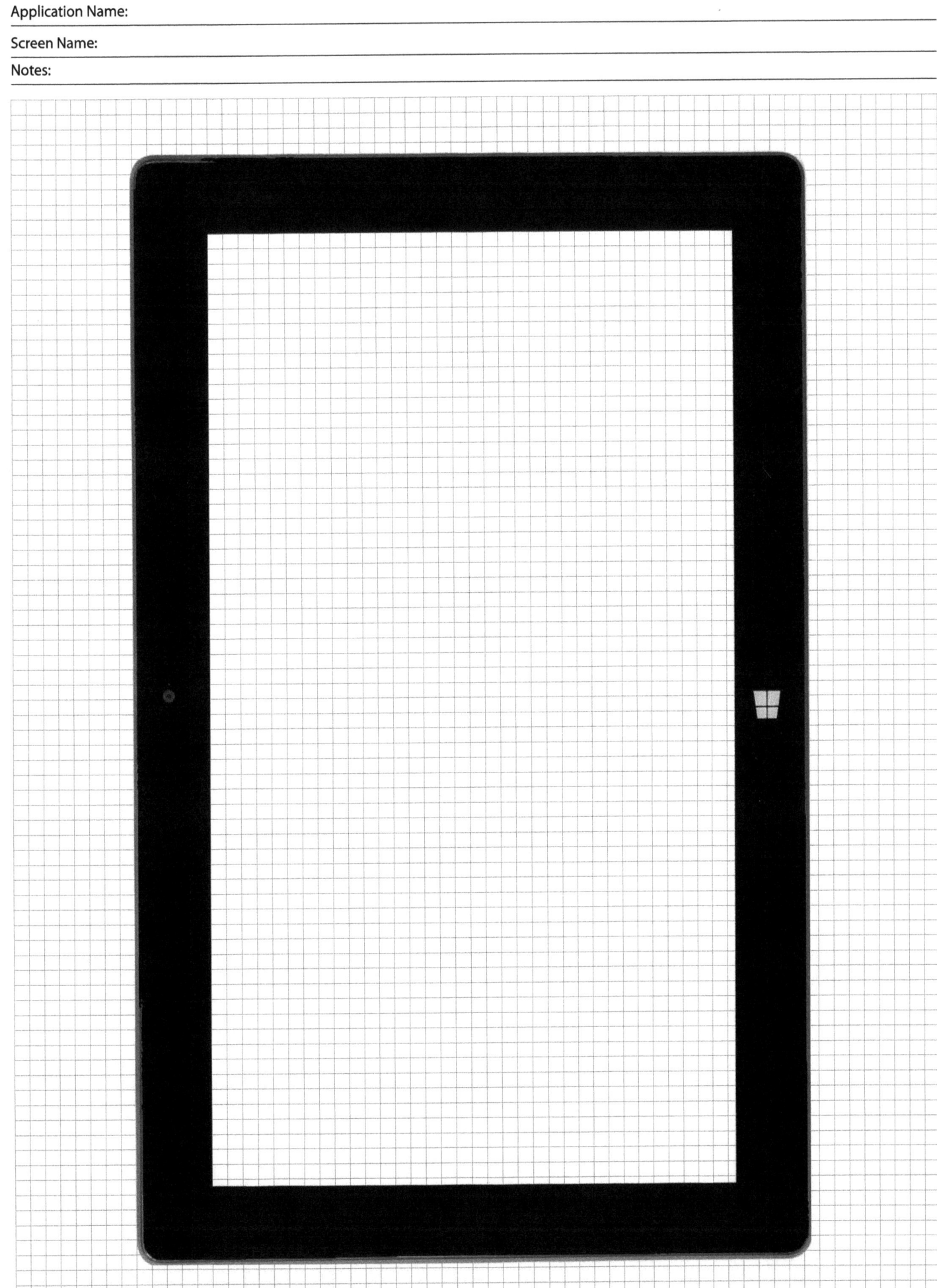

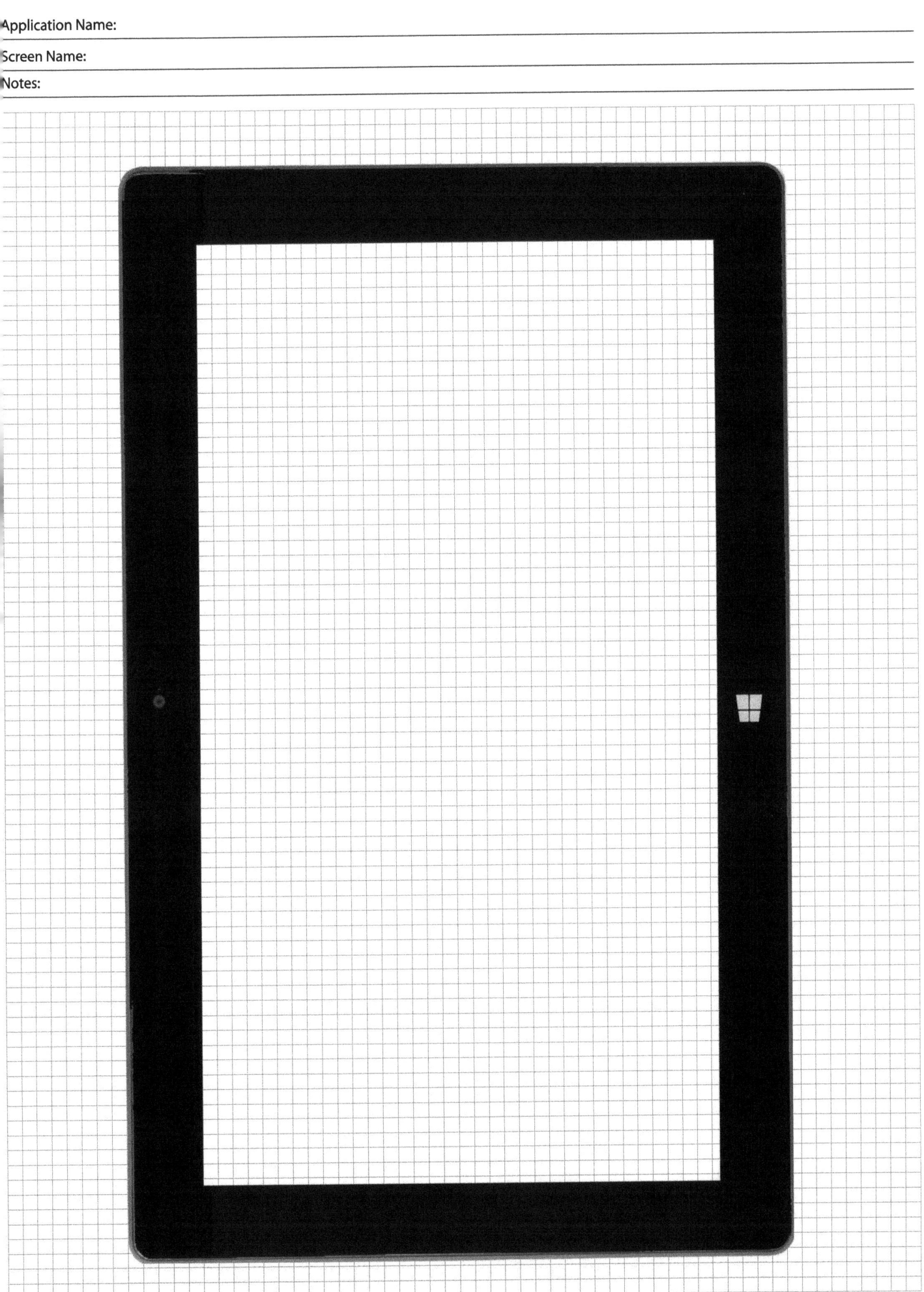

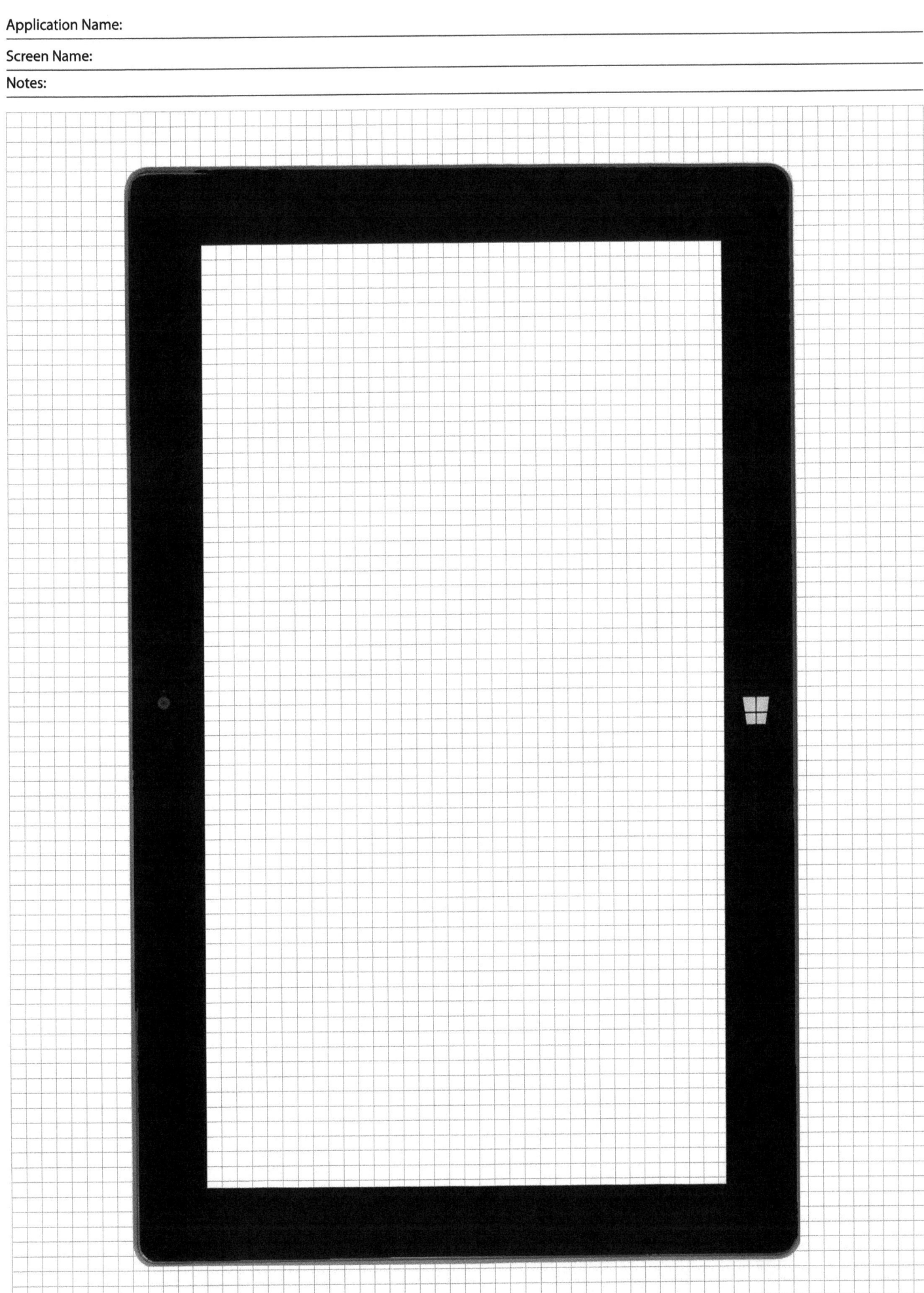

Application Name:

Screen Name:

Notes:

Application Name:

Screen Name:

Notes:

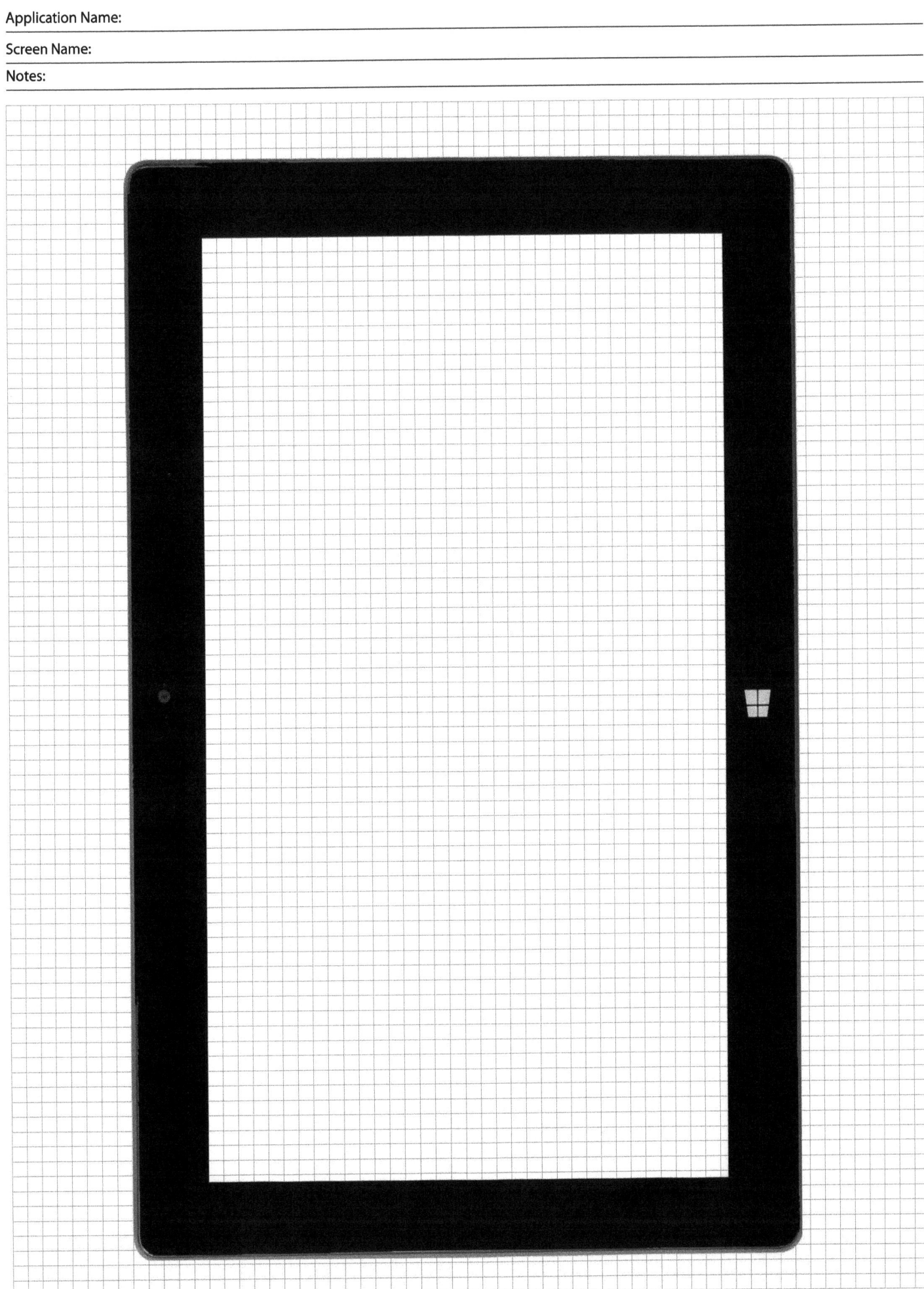

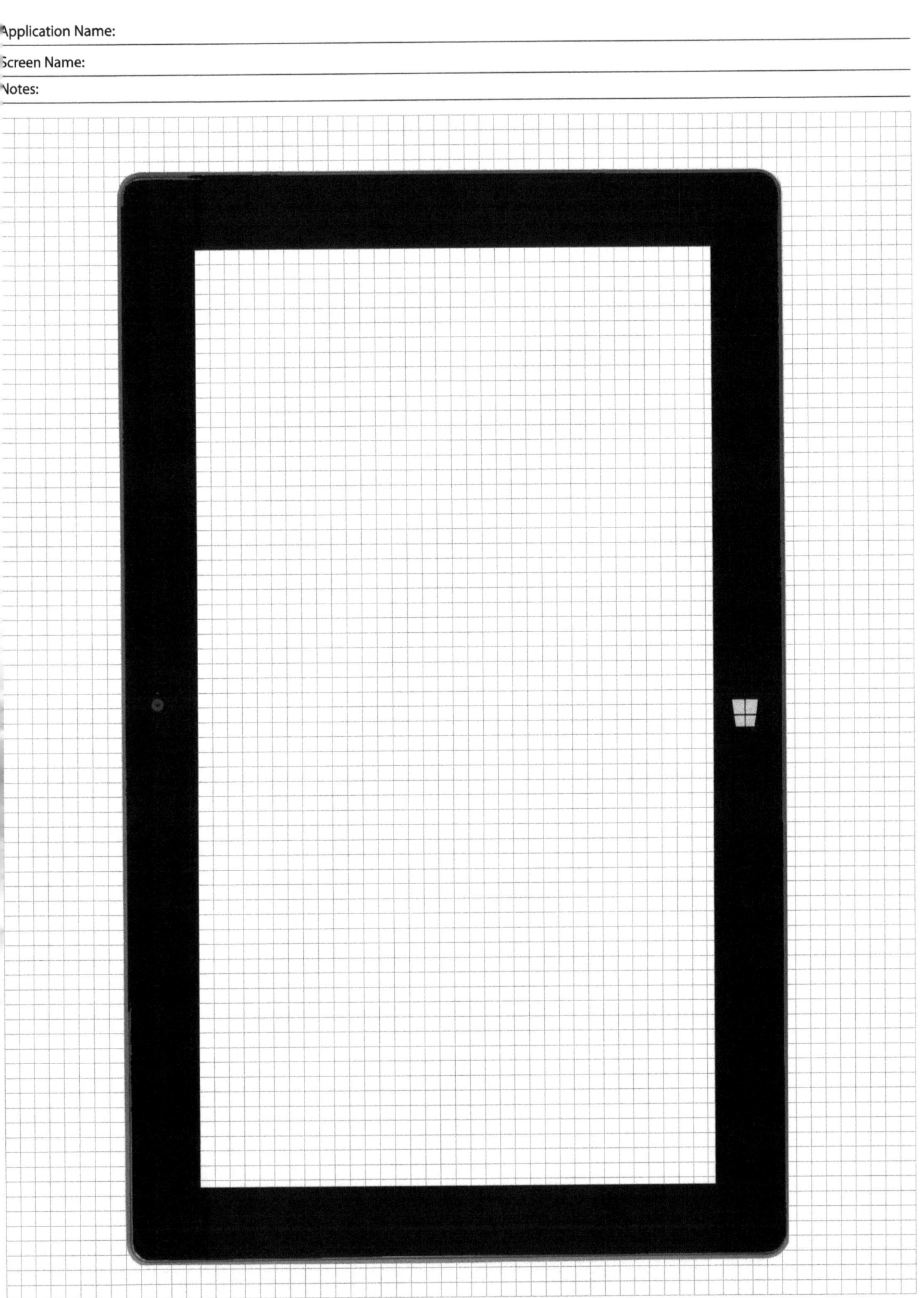

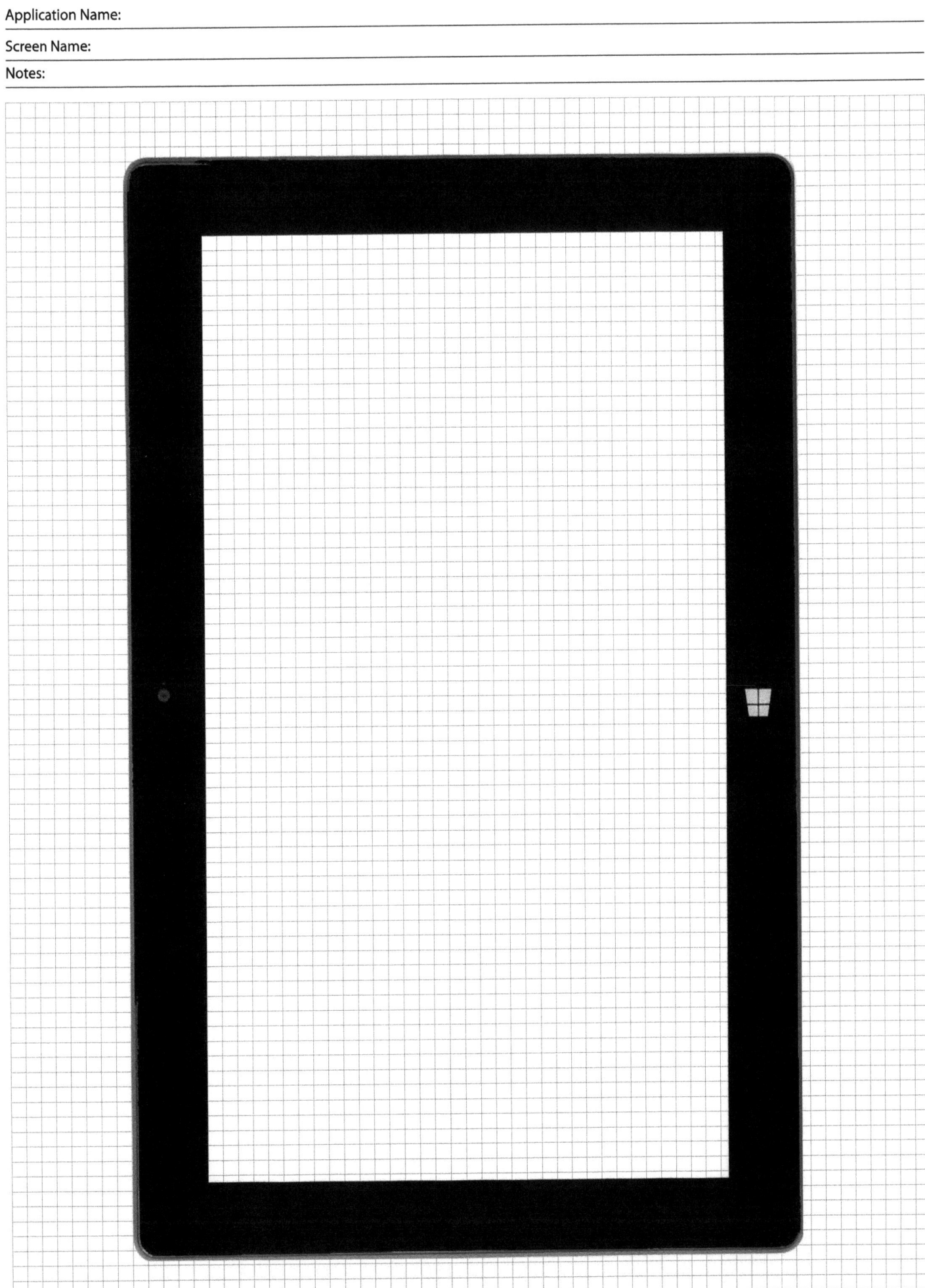

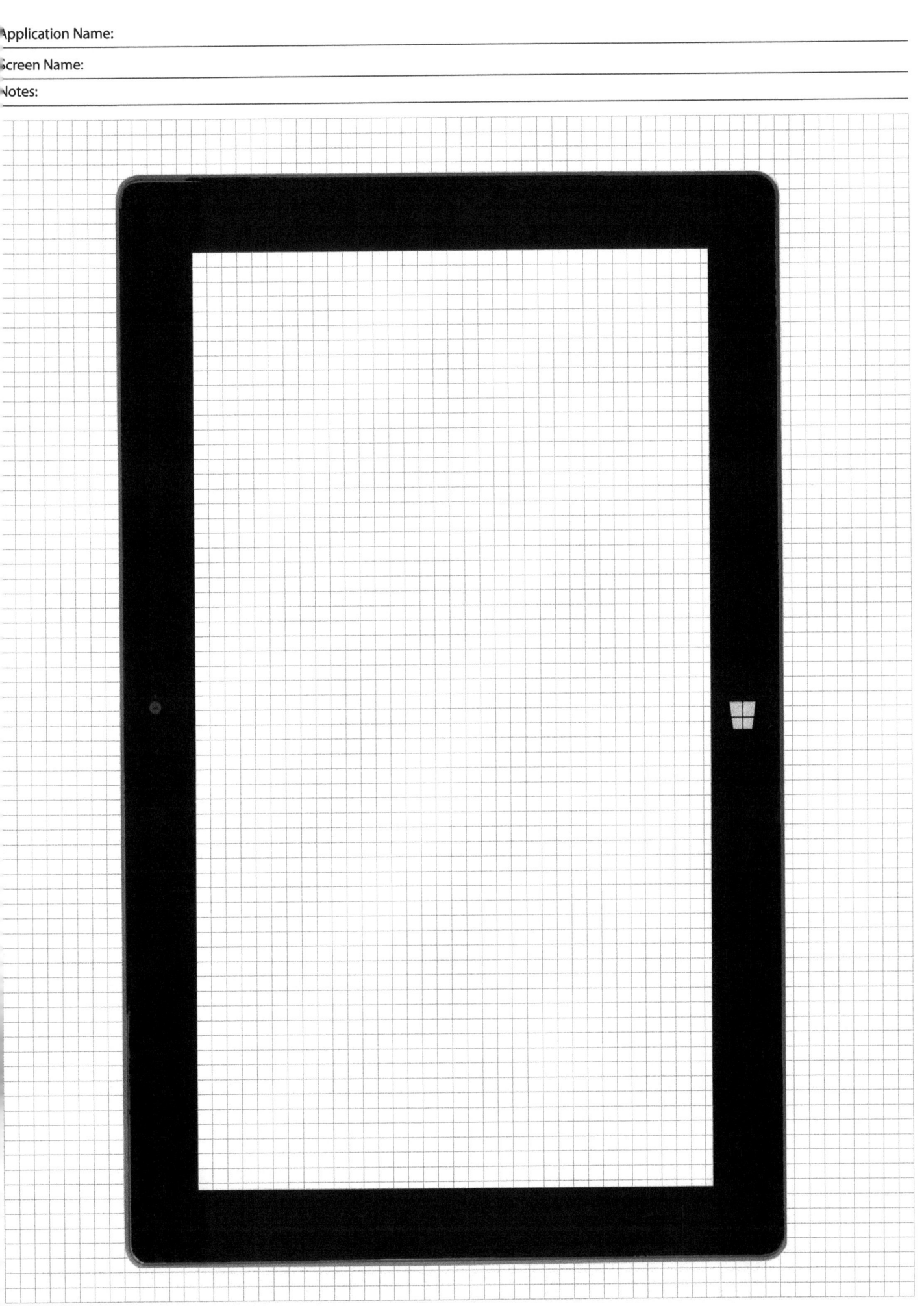

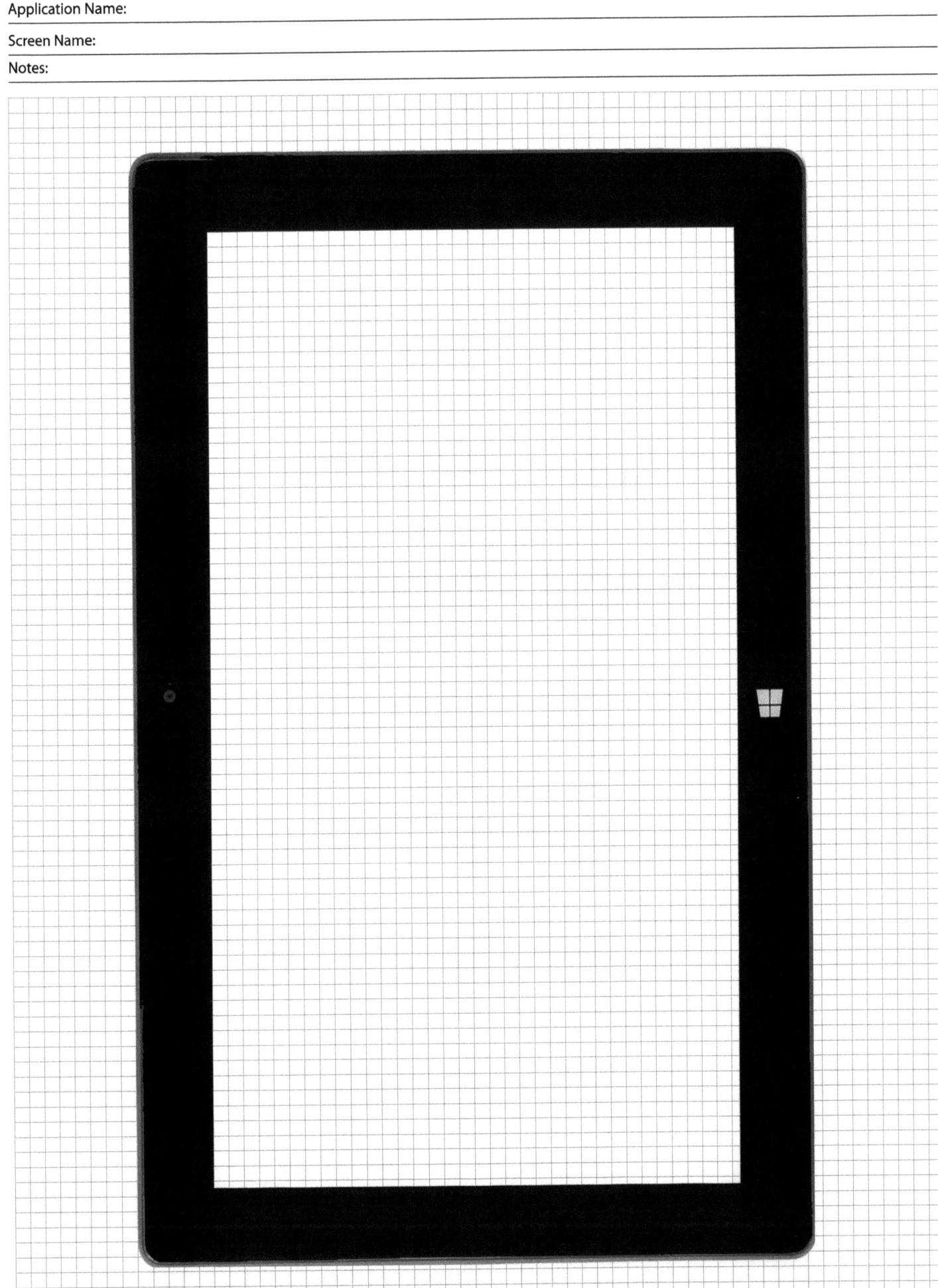

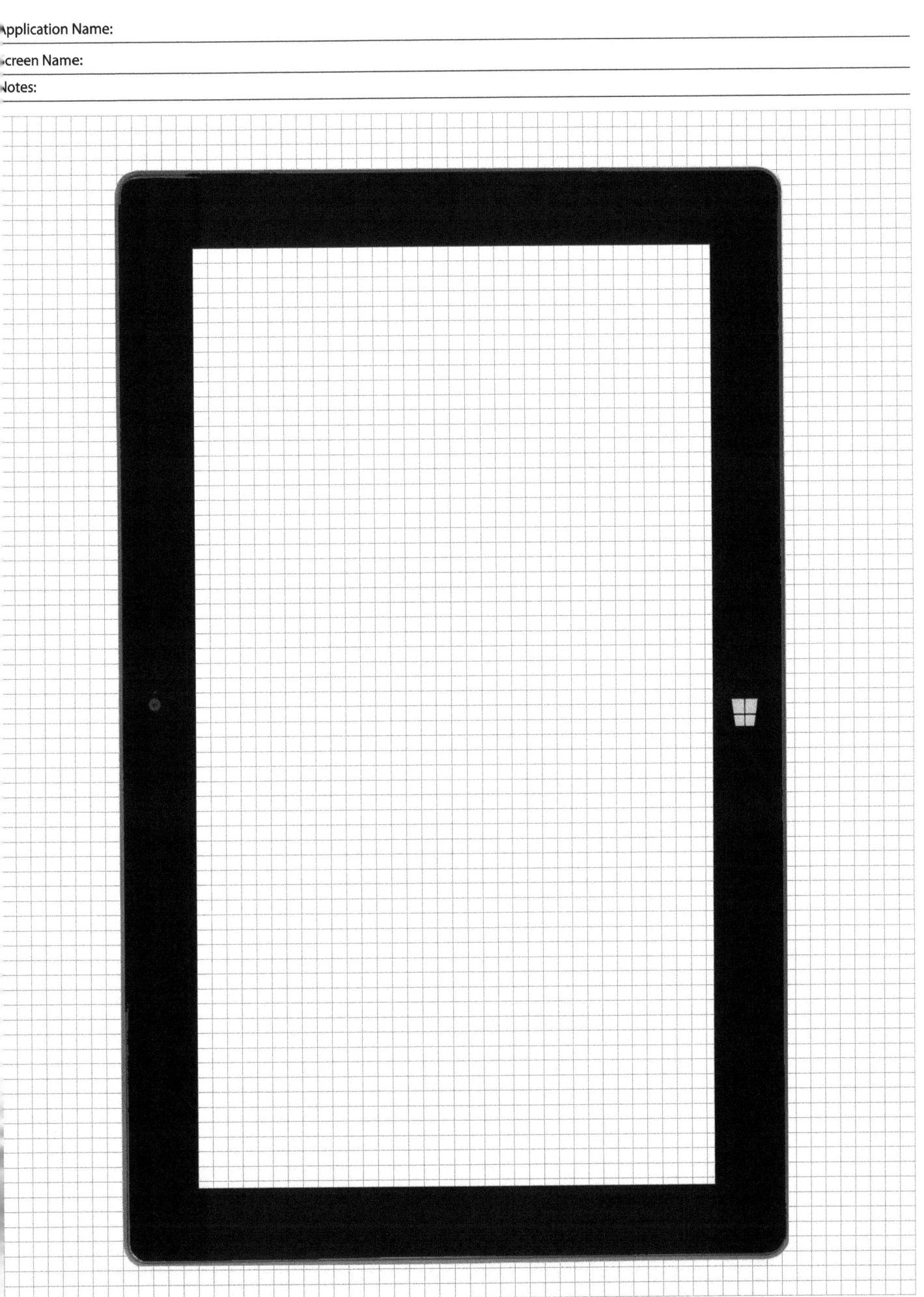

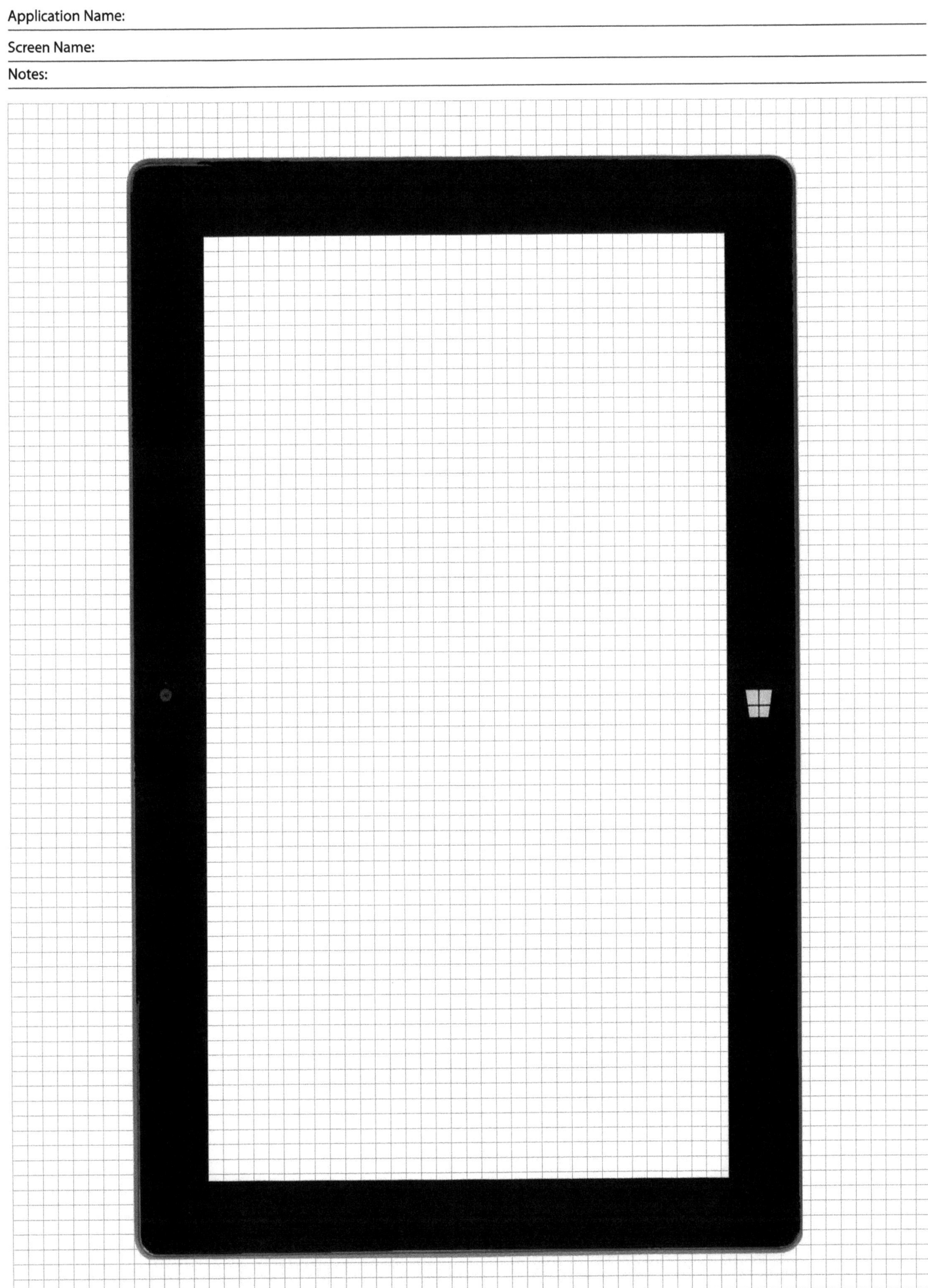

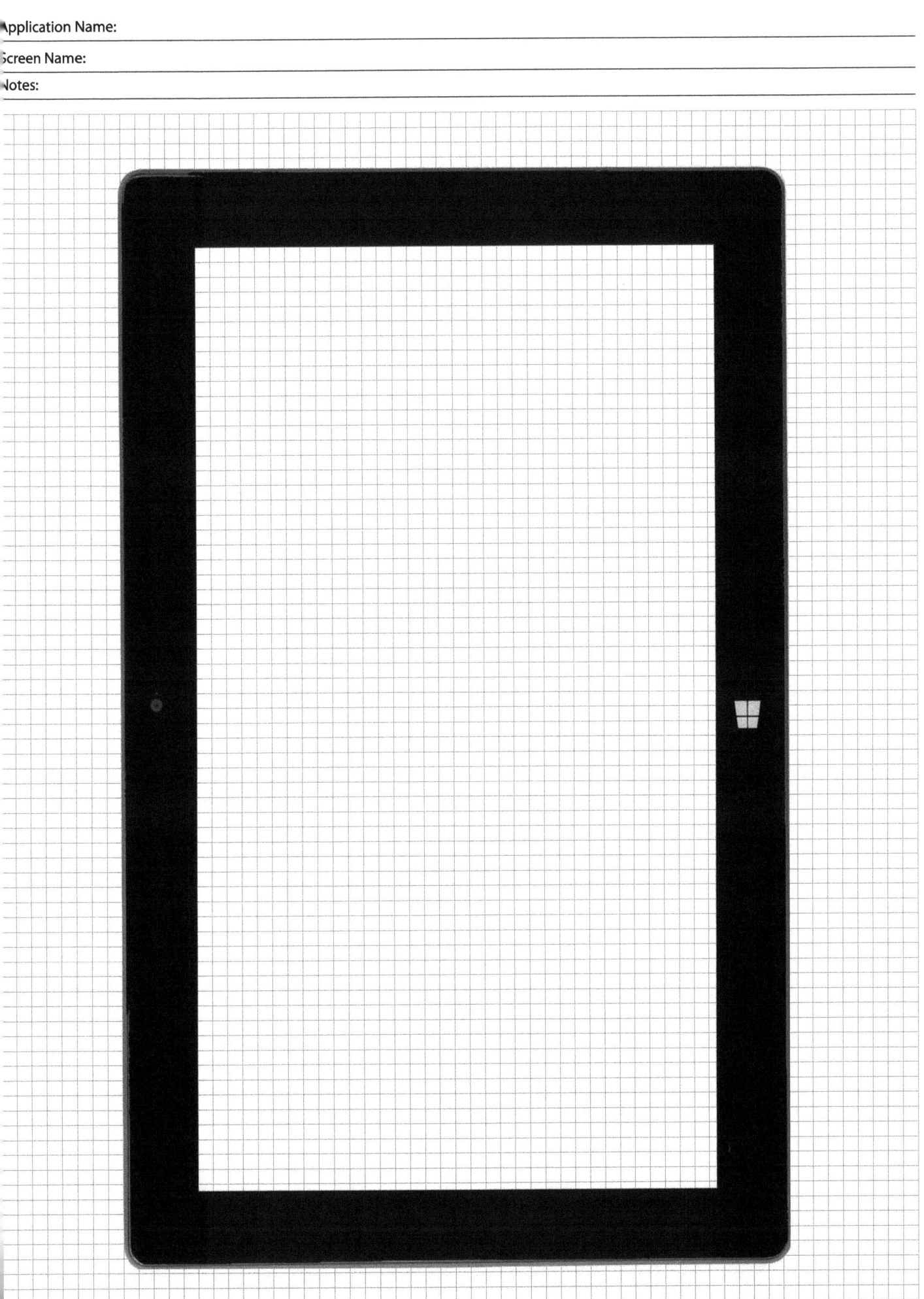

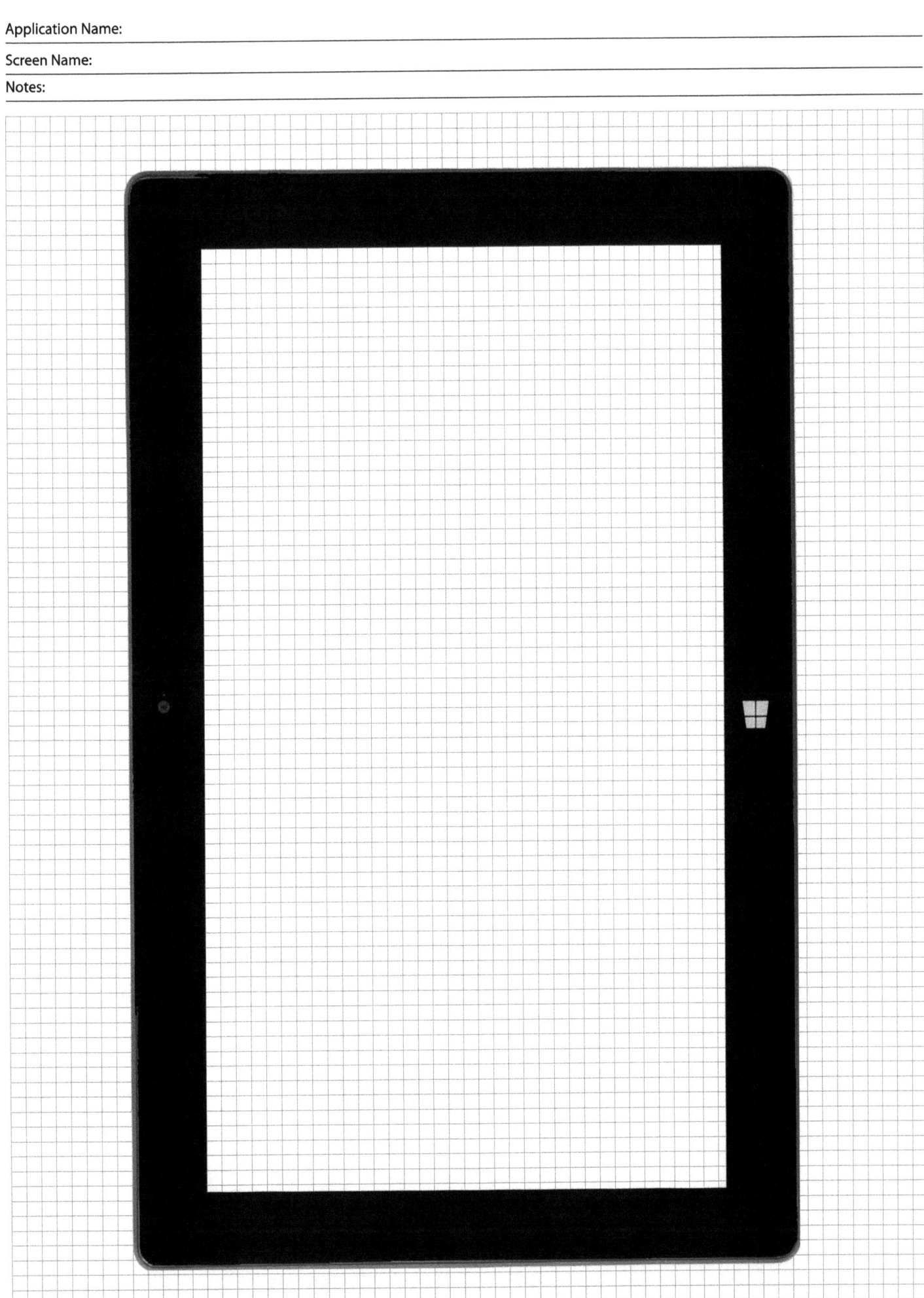

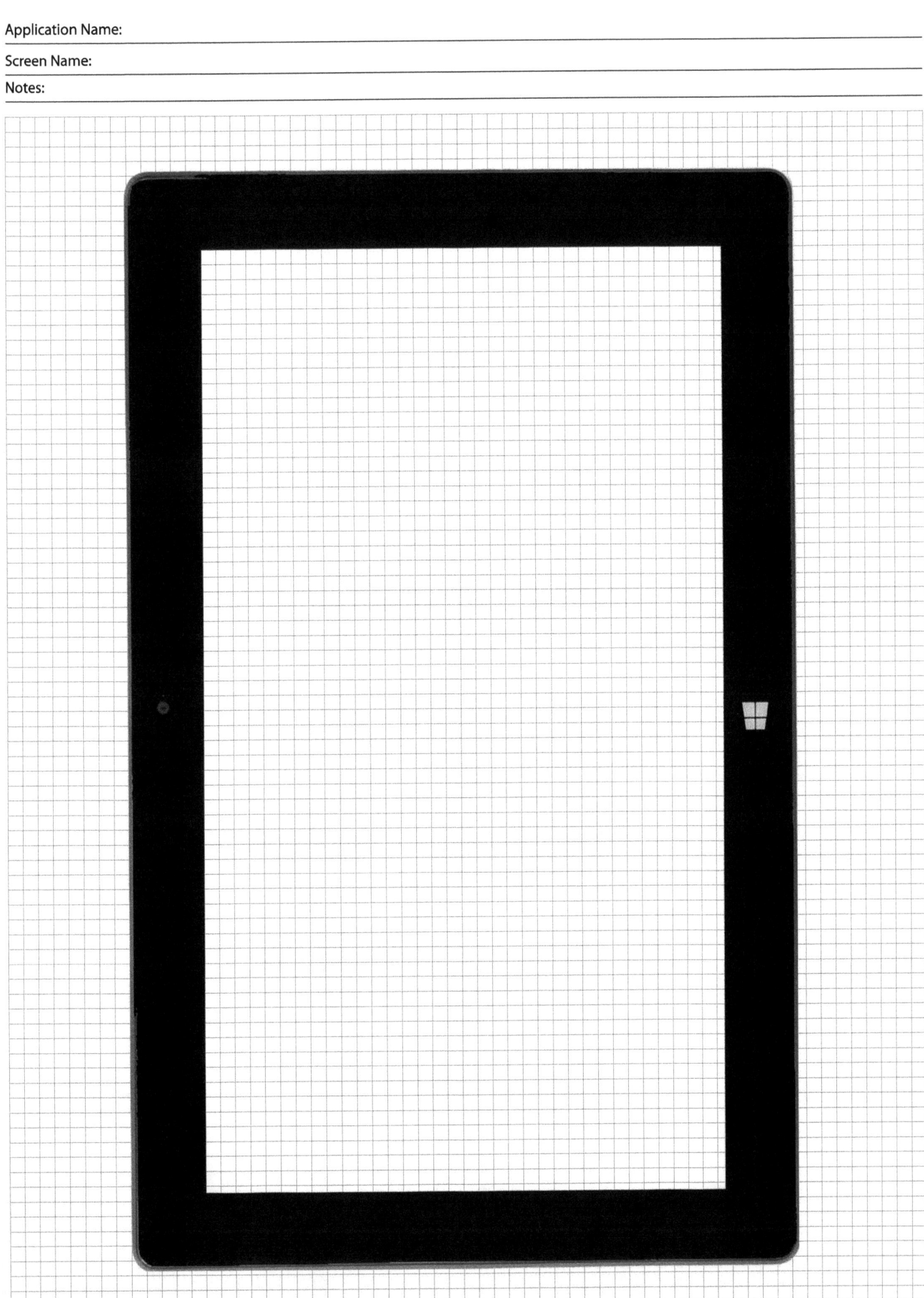

www.ingramcontent.com/pod-product-compliance
Ingram Content Group UK Ltd.
Pitfield, Milton Keynes, MK11 3LW, UK
UKHW052128231225
466357UK00015B/253